Shafer
VINEYARDS

Line on Wine

FACTS, FIGURES AND FUN FROM THE
INTERNATIONAL WORLD OF WINE

RESEARCHED, WRITTEN AND EDITED BY ANDY DEMSKY

BOOK DESIGN: MICHAEL KAVISH

ILLUSTRATIONS:
3,800 EARLY ADVERTISING CUTS, CAROL BELANGER GRAFTON,
DOVER PUBLICATIONS, INC.
FOOD AND DRINK, A PICTORIAL ARCHIVE FROM NINETEENTH-CENTURY SOURCES,
JIM HARTER, DOVER PUBLICATIONS, INC.
BRAUN & SCHNEIDER'S HISTORIC COSTUME, DOVER PUBLICATIONS, INC.

PRINTING: BANTA BOOK GROUP

FIRST EDITION

PRINTED IN CHINA

Shafer
VINEYARDS
Line on Wine®

FACTS, FIGURES AND FUN FROM THE
INTERNATIONAL WORLD OF WINE

SEE SHAFER PUBLISH

Some things are inescapable. For me it's publishing, apparently. Prior to our family's life in a Napa Valley vineyard I spent many years in Chicago helping to produce and promote textbooks for school children. A few of you may still remember my old favorites, the Dick and Jane basic readers.

While all that is 30 years in the past, my family and I find ourselves once again involved in creating books intended to educate and entertain. For ten years *Line on Wine*® has been a postcard of obscure wine-related facts that we mailed three times a year to our in-house customer and media lists. Over the years the thing has gained a following, the list has grown, and after a decade the idea came along to create a *Line on Wine* book.

We've produced this little volume to share the joy we take in the multifaceted world of wine – the science, art and even goofiness – and wish you a fun and rewarding reading experience.

— John Shafer, Chairman, Shafer Vineyards

SNIFFING OUT THE WIT IN WINE

Humor and wine have never been particularly comfortable together in this country. Simply stated, we take wine too seriously. Have you ever heard anyone say, "I like string beans but I don't understand them." Perhaps not, but people are always saying that about wine. Wine intimidates most of us. In Europe, wine stories, wine songs, even wine jokes, are common coin. Europeans and wine are, of course, old friends; here, we're just getting to know each other.

We are insecure when it comes to wine, which means we are vulnerable. A legion of self-help gurus swarm around us, brandishing books and magazines, CDs and videos, all guaranteed to make us experts overnight. I'm not sure which is worse for wine, pedantry or too much oak. We do need help, a lot of us. What we lack are simple guideposts which forget lesson plans and suggest, light-heartedly, that sticking one's nose in a glass and frowning is not the only way to wine pleasure. The Shafers' little book is just such a guidepost. It recognizes our serious side but it tickles our fancy as well. It promises "Facts, Figures and Fun."

It notes, matter-of-factly, that Luxembourg leads the world in per capita wine consumption at 63.33 liters per Luxemburger per year, while the United States, with a measly 7.69 liters per head, ranks 34th, just ahead of fun-loving Latvia. Then, a bit more nonchalantly, it discloses that a spa in Ontario, Canada will massage you with honey and chardonnay. (It might have noted that there are chardonnays fit for little else, but that's not the Shafer style.) One of my favorite items reveals that an unnamed British supermarket chain has insured its wine buyer's tongue for $17-million. Amusing, yes, but thought-provoking, too. If I don't like their Beaujolais, can I file a claim?

You will learn important stuff here, like how Air New Zealand lightens its planes, what Australians call their dessert wines and whether the rain in Spain really does fall mostly on the plain. Not as important as, for example, the difference between Balling and Brix, or between Santa Rosa and St. Emilion but certainly more fun.

Most winery newsletters follow a similar pattern: they are relentlessly folksy and they plug the wines. The Shafer *Line on Wine* is a newsletter, sort of. It comes from a winery and it comes regularly, three times a year. But there the resemblance ends. There is nothing about the new winemaker, the new puppies or the old zinfandel vines; just a witty gathering of brief items about the world of wine — some intriguing, some mildly interesting, some just plain goofy.

Some years ago, when I first encountered the *Line on Wine* cards, I said to John Shafer. "You ought to put these in a book," knowing that no one ever takes my advice on anything. He fooled me. I'm happy that he did.

— *Frank Prial, Wine Columnist,* The New York Times

A new study tells us that moderate wine drinking
can protect your brain from what age-related malady?

Dementia

Newsday

In the 1850s, what place in California grew
ten times as many grapes as Napa Valley?

Los Angeles

Napa Valley Vintners

The small Montana town of Malta offers a yearly festival for
which your entry fee gets you wine tasting and:

The chance to examine that year's trove of locally discovered dinosaur bones

Great Falls Tribune

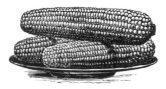

Move over corn, what state has eight wineries
with five more expected to open?

Nebraska

Omaha World-Herald

The oldest winery in the Americas was established where in 1597?

The northern Mexico town of Parras de la Fuente

Associated Press

A 13th-century French decree banished what
along Burgundy's famous Cote d'Or?

The Gamay grape

Telegraph.co.uk

Napa Valley is 1/8th the size of what other
wine producing region?

Bordeaux

Napa Valley Vintners

George Lucas, creator of the Star Wars movie series, has become a
California vintner selling a Merlot and Chardonnay under the
brand name "Viandante del Cielo," which in Italian means:

Sky walker

SciFi.com

In Britain women between the ages of 18 and 25, on average, get
through the equivalent of how many bottles of wine a week?

Five

Telegraph.co.uk

The Greek word symposium means, literally:

The act of drinking [wine] together

OpenDemocracy.net

Number of yeast cells in one drop of fermenting grape juice:

5 million   *Knowing & Making Wine, E. Peynaud*

The most visited winery in the United States is located where?

Asheville, North Carolina, where Biltmore Estate Winery claims to host more than 1 million guests each year

The Business Journal (Greensboro, NC)

Some do and some don't.
43 percent of American adults don't do what?

Imbibe alcohol at all   *San Francisco Chronicle*

In 2002 what wine expanded its lead in
sales over Cabernet in the U.S.?

Merlot   *Motto, Kryla, Fisher, LLP*

A new fining agent for wine developed in New Zealand
is made from what part of a hoki fish?

Its skin

New Zealand Press Association

Florida's 14 wineries turn what locally dominant
grape into 300,000 gallons of wine a year?

Muscadine

Palm Beach Post

A bakery in Texas brightened the holidays for consumers
who are both wine enthusiasts and lovers of very dense
snacks by announcing the best wines to pair with:

Fruitcake
(Off-dry white and off-dry sparkling)

PR Newswire

25 percent of sparkling wine and Champagne is sold when?

In the two weeks leading up to Christmas

Oakland Tribune

There are now how many licensed wineries in Illinois?

39

(up from nine in 1997)   *The Southern Illinoisian*

Shafer Vineyards will still be producing
Hillside Select in what year?

2026

According to Sci-fi novel *Step Into Chaos*, William Shatner (Chapter 13, subchapter 1)

Date of the first known vintage produced in California:

1782   *California Wine*

Percentage of American households not owning a corkscrew:

50%

Barron's

True or False: The rain in Spain falls mainly on the plain.

False

***(Spain's largest plain, La Mancha, is hot, drought-prone and
produces white wines mainly destined for distillation.)***

The Belfast Telegraph

Farmers in Lebanon's Bekaa Valley are giving up
what traditional crop to raise wine grapes?

Hashish

Financial Times (London)

Research shows that drinking wine combats a bacterium called
H. pylori, which translates into fewer cases of what?

Ulcers

WineSpectator.com

"… SO MUCH THE WORSE FOR THOSE WHO FEAR
WINE, FOR IT IS BECAUSE THEY HAVE BAD
THOUGHTS WHICH THEY ARE AFRAID THE LIQUOR
WILL EXTRACT FROM THEIR HEARTS."

— *Alexandre Dumas, The Count of Monte Cristo*

A French law, which dates to 1951, stipulates that bottles of Beaujolais Nouveau wine may be made available for consumption when?

Each year on the third Thursday of November
(More than 65 million cases of Beaujolais Nouveau
are released around the world.) The Baltimore Sun

Bulgaria's native red grape varietals:

Gamza, Mavrud and Melnik The Belfast Telegraph

Thousands of bottles of wine from the palace cellar of Romania's former dictator Nicolae Ceausescu were thrown away by housekeepers to make storage space for what?

Cleaning equipment Ananova.com

Wine imports to India currently stand at 250,000 cases,
while whisky makers bring into the country:

55 million cases *The Telegraph (Calcutta)*

Until around 1945, wines from Burgundy and
Champagne often came in:

800ml bottles *About.com*

Alcohol, such as that in wine, raises and lowers what?

It increases HDL, "good" cholesterol, and reduces LDL, "bad" cholesterol *Better Nutrition*

In the U.S., the average time between the purchase of a bottle of wine and the consumption of that bottle is:

Four hours

Lodi News-Sentinel

Ancient Mesopotamian and Egyptian winemakers saved their wares in:

Amphorae — clay flasks

About.com

80 percent of all wines sold in the U.S. cost:

$10 or less

Lodi News-Sentinel

New Zealand's Central Otago wine country claims what distinction?

It is the southernmost wine growing region in the world (Latitude 45° South)

Media.NewZealand.com

The Kansas City Chiefs football team came under fire from
the National Football League when the team's coach offered
a kicker what if he could complete a field goal?

A bottle of Napa Valley Cabernet Sauvignon

Wine Spectator

According to a poll in Britain, nearly 6 out of 10
questioned don't fancy doing what?

Buying a screw-top bottle of wine

Telegraph.co.uk

With what are some Australian winemakers replacing
their stainless steel fermentation tanks?

Large plastic bags

Wines & Vines

Women account for only 17 percent of customers where?

Fine wine stores

FineWine.com

A supermarket chain in England has insured the
tongue of its chief wine buyer for:

10 million pounds (about $17.3 million)

Wine Spectator.com

Canada's second largest market for ice wine after the U.S. is:

Taiwan
(Fake ice wines hold about a 50 percent market share)

Taiwan News

Grapes are tied with what other agricultural product
for the sixth most valuable crop in the U.S.?

Potatoes   *WineSpectator.com*

An Internet retailer now offers a kit of
bad wine smells which include:

**_Brett, Corked, Garlic/Onion, Geranium,
Maderized, Nail Polish Remover, Oxidized,
Rotten Eggs, Sulfur, Sweet Corn, Unripe, Vinegar_**

The Buffalo News

In 2002 U.S. wineries sold 595 million gallons of wine.
That's equal to what other liquid statistic?

**_The amount of waste water
that Los Angeles treats in a day_**

Wine Institute & National Society of Professional Engineers (nspe.org)

In an era before the use of corks, how did ancient Romans
preserve their wines from oxidation?

**_By floating a layer of olive oil
at the top of their storage vessels_** *WinePros.org*

Opened wine stored in the refrigerator lasts how much longer than opened wine stored at room temperature?

Six to 16 times longer *The Alchemist's Wine Perspective*

The "backbone" of English viticulture is a varietal called:

Müller-Thurgau (also known as Rivaner)

EnglishWineProducers.com

Advanced wine cellar software now tells wine lovers when to do what?

Drink their aging reds *The Oregonian*

Air travelers in Canada have been warned that confiscated items can include:

Fruitcake and bottles of homemade wine

Canadian Broadcasting Corporation

"WITH MIRTH AND LAUGHTER LET
OLD WRINKLES COME, AND LET MY LIVER RATHER
HEAT WITH WINE THAN MY HEART COOL WITH
MORTIFYING GROANS."

— *Shakespeare,* Merchant of Venice

We know that reducing the size of harvest picking bins delivers grapes in better condition to the crush pad. Who else benefits?

Farm workers, who report reduced ergonomic injuries

Ergoweb.com

Australians call their fortified dessert wines:

Stickies

The New York Times

A vintner in Russia now offers that country's first what?

Plum wine

(Sales have been so good — more than 2 million bottles per year — that the winery plans to roll out bilberry, apricot, mango and chokeberry wines as well.)

The St. Petersburg Times

Along the shores of Lake Malawi, Africa,
red wine is made from what local fruit?

A forest berry called misuku. White wines are made from oranges, guavas, bananas and peaches

African Eye News Service

North Carolina has been awarded its first what?

American Viticultural Area (AVA) — Yadkin Valley

The Business Journal (Greensboro, NC)

For wine lovers with stuffed-up noses a new product promises to
restore full olfactory prowess through the magic of:

A nasal rinse *The National Association of American Wineries*

In ancient times up through the Middle Ages wine was drunk as a safe alternative to what other thirst quencher?

Water, which was often contaminated   *BBC*

Researchers in South Africa say hangover headaches are caused by:

Bioamines, which come from the bacteria responsible for setting off malolactic fermentation

Decanter.com

In China, wine is often mixed with what?

Sprite
(Or other popular soft drinks and pieces of fruit)

The New York Times

Makers of a new PDA-based wine guide say it offers hand-held users how many wine ratings at the touch of a button?

53,000

Scotsman.com

U.S. consumers spend how much each year on wines from Europe?

$2 billion

New York Post

Goblets unearthed in China now suggest that winemaking there dates back:

5,000 years

Chinaview.cn

A Washington state winery saw sales of one of its wines quadruple after changing the name from:

Pinot Gris to Pinot Grigio

The Daily Herald (Everett, Washington)

There are now around 10 companies in California
devoted exclusively to what?

Wine cave construction   San Francisco Chronicle

How long have winemakers been adding sulfites to wines?

More than 2,000 years
***(The Greeks and Romans used sulfur candles to sterilize
their wine barrels and amphorae. Sulfur keeps wine clear
by preventing organisms from growing in the wine.)***   About.com

The title of world's oldest winery is claimed by:

*Barone Ricasoli. The Tuscan Ricasoli family
first purchased their land in 1141 A.D.*

GlobalGourmet.com

An inventor claims to have eliminated the need to
aerate wine thanks to what?

A straw with a hole in the side   Wine Spectator

"TAKE WINE AWAY ...
AND EVERY OTHER HUMAN JOY IS DEAD."

— *Euripides*

A new product, which clips onto the neck of a wine bottle, promises to age wine instantly through the wonder of:

Magnets

PR Newswire

Resveratrol in red wine appears to reduce the amount of harmful chemicals in the lungs that causes what ?

Respiratory illness

TheAge.com

True or False: Wine consumption in the U.S. has more than doubled in the last 12 years.

True

The New York Times

According to French researchers, red wine picks up potential cancer-fighting compounds from:

Oak barrels

ScientificAmerican.com

True or False: Wine consumption among India's one billion people stands at 2 bottles per capita.

False. It is .006
(Worldwide that number is 5 bottles)

MSNBC.com

An extract of red wine is now being used to kill yeasts, molds and fungi that shorten the life of your favorite what?

Fruit

New Scientist

The longest time a no-sulfite-added wine
can survive is estimated to be.

18 months

About.com

Grape growers in Connecticut report that a major
source of vine damage comes from what culprit?

Wild turkeys

Wine Business Monthly

Winery-owning descendants of the poet Dante,
author of *The Divine Comedy*, recently released a special
wine to celebrate which anniversary?

Their 650th

Haaretz.com (Israel)

Scientists say the world's oldest wine was produced by whom?

**Stone Age vintners in the former
Soviet Republic of Georgia 8,000 years ago**

Independent (London)

On Dec. 5, 1933, 14 years of Prohibition came to an end when what state became the 36th state to ratify the 21st Amendment?

Utah

(The 21st Amendment gives states authority to regulate their own alcohol sales.) San Francisco Chronicle

It is believed that wine grapes have been grown in France's Rhône region since:

Around 125 B.C. Business Day (New Zealand)

In 2002 per capita wine consumption rose in every U.S. state. Which state led the charge?

Tennessee, up almost 13 percent

Dan Berger's Vintage Experiences

Forest management was first instituted in France when?

The late 1200s Wine Business Monthly

Average number of useful harvests
a cork tree will yield in its lifetime:

15

Italcork

The world's highest elevation vineyard is located in Argentina at:

9,892 ft

Jancisrobinson.com

Russian submariners are sometimes served red wine
to help deal with what on-the-job hazard?

Radiation sickness

Agence France Presse

Of all the wood harvested in France's prime oak forests
where wine barrel materials are sourced,
what percentage becomes furniture?

90

Wine Business Monthly

What technology now gauges the
moisture content of soils in vineyards?

Radar

CNN.com

A group of French winegrowers sued the French weather
forecasting service for what?

Not warning them of a hailstorm

Wines & Vines

New York state produces eight million cases of wine,
but only about 15 percent is from:

The species vinifera

Ithaca Journal

Red wines accounted for 17 percent of the U.S. market
in 1991 and how much ten years later?

Almost 40

Air New Zealand has announced it will lower the weight
of its planes and significantly cut fuel costs by:

Offering wine in plastic bottles instead of heavier glass

True or False: All calories in wine come from alcohol.

True
(74 calories in 3.5 ounces of red wine and 70 calories in white)

New bioterrorism rules require U.S. wineries to:

Register with the Food and Drug Administration

"THE BEST USE OF BAD WINE
IS TO DRIVE AWAY POOR RELATIONS."

— *French proverb*

Research now suggests that the life-extending
benefits of a low-calorie diet has been duplicated
by what element in red wine?

Resveratrol   Dan Berger's Vintage Experiences

It is Jewish tradition to put a small amount of wine on the
tongues of week-old boys to dull the pain of what?

Circumcision   San Francisco Chronicle

Age of the grape vine reported to be the world's oldest,
located in Maribor, Slovenia:

400 years   The Wine News

Pyrazene is the chemical compound that can give
Cabernet a what characteristic?

Herbal

Dan Berger's Vintage Experiences

Percentage of volume of a cork occupied by gases
(nitrogen and oxygen):

85

Knowing & Making Wine, E. Peynaud

Recently French magazine *Lyon Mag* was fined about
$100,000 for characterizing the French appellation
Beaujolais as producing what?

Vin de merde (crappy wine)

The Independent (London)

French wine promoters are working in Taiwan to encourage the pairing of French Reislings and Champagnes with what local dishes?

Sea cucumber and spicy eel   *ETaiwanNews.com*

Percentage of wines in the 2001 San Diego Wine Competition that were corked:

3.3   *Wine Business Insider*

With more than 1,400 brands, this country has more wine brands per capita than any other:

Australia   *Dan Berger's Vintage Experiences*

Number of cases of wine a home winemaker could legally produce per year during prohibition:

83   *The Wine Institute*

True or False: Tokay produced in Australia comes from the same grape as that made in Hungary.

False

(The Aussie wine is vinted from muscadelle.)

The New York Times

The wine Thomas Jefferson and colleagues drank to toast the new Declaration of Independence:

Madeira

The Wine News

In winemaking parlance the adding of sugar during fermentation to increase alcohol content is called what?

Chaptalization

Agence France-Presse

Length of time Pierce's disease has been present in California:

Over 100 years

Pressdemocrat.com

Percentage of wine purchases in U.S.
supermarkets that are made by women:

72 *Vineyard & Winery Management*

Old vine Zinfandel just got really old. One California winery
offers a Zin that it claims comes from vines that date back to:

1869 *PRNewswire.com*

Napa Valley crop described in an 1889 newspaper
as the finest of its kind grown in the United States:

Hops *Napa Valley Register*

The Guadalupe Valley, located 10 miles east of the Baja beach town of Ensenada, is touted as Mexico's new what?

Wine country

(Where wine has been produced since the 1880s) <small>Cox News Service</small>

The number of vineyards in Pennsylvania has increased by what percent since 1989?

79

(Its 84 wineries ranks the state fifth in the nation in number of wineries.) <small>Associated Press</small>

Type of oak barrels preferred by premium Bordeaux wineries prior to World War II:

Hungarian <small>Vineyard and Winery Management</small>

Combined cork harvest in Portugal and Spain:

250,000 tons <small>Winesandvines.com</small>

Recent DNA tests conducted in France have shown the grapes Dureza and Mondeuse Blanche to be the parents of:

Syrah

Quarterly Review of Wines

Era when labels first appeared on wine bottles:

Early 1700s

Decade when suitable glue was developed
to hold labels on bottles:

1860s

Wines & Vines

The Burgundian equivalent to the double
magnum used for Bordeaux wines:

Jeroboam

Santé

"TO KNOW THE VINTAGE AND QUALITY OF A WINE
ONE NEED NOT DRINK THE WHOLE CASK."

— *Oscar Wilde*

American wine drinkers consume the most wine on this day:

Thanksgiving

St. Helena Star

Of the $20 billion Americans spent on wine in 2000, this percentage was spent on California wine:

72

Napa Valley Wine Library Report

Location of the only tourist-based agricultural economy in California:

Napa County

sfgate.com

Amount of grapes a vineyard worker can harvest in a good day:

Two tons

St. Helena Star

Annual per capita consumption of wine in France in 1960:

100 liters
Today: 55 liters

Independent Online

Winning more medals than any other region in the U.S., Napa Valley first established its reputation at this event in Paris:

1889 World's Fair

St. Helena Star

In Bulgaria, February 14 is not a day of hearts and flowers, but instead marks a traditional celebration of:

Winemaking, called the Feast of St. Trifon

Sofia News Agency

Occupying over 1 million acres in Spain, this is the world's most planted grape:

Airén

Quarterly Review of Wines

Number of bird species dependent on the cork oak trees of Spain and Portugal:

42

Guardian Weekly (London)

Made undrinkable by the required addition of salt, cooking sherry produced during Prohibition was made palatable with this technique:

Adding peeled potatoes

St. Helena Star

Water accounts for this percentage of wine's content:

86

While individual flavor elements comprise:

2%

The Quarterly Review of Wines

Age of cork tree at first harvest of wine-quality cork:

45 years

Napa Valley Register

Speed at which a Champagne cork exits the bottle:

40 m.p.h.

Santé

Number of minutes a grape can endure at 31°F before freezing:

30

Plain Talk About Fine Wine, J. Meyer

First nation in the world to use appellation labeling on wines:

Greece

Wine & Spirits

Average yield from a ton of grapes.

170 gallons

Dan Berger's Vintage Experiences

Center of California's grape growing during the mid-1800s:

Southern California

Center of California's wine sales and consumption at that time:
San Francisco

Wine Spectator

Percentage of wine made each year throughout
the world that's consumed before the next harvest:

95

Wine & Spirits

Average price for Napa Cabernet grapes in the 2003 harvest:

$4,010 per ton   *Napa County Agricultural Crop Report*

Approximate number of nights per year frost
protection is needed in Napa or Sonoma Counties:

Six

Lake County (Napa's northern neighbor): 12 – 18

University of California at Davis & U.S. Dept of Agriculture

Number of years between harvests of a cork tree's bark:

10   *Italcork*

Recently discovered Vatican documents point to this spot as the birthplace of sparkling wine:

Montepulciano, Italy

Epicurissimo.com

First known reference to a specific wine vintage was made by the Roman historian Pliny the Elder, who rated this vintage as one "of the highest excellence."

121 B.C.

Age of above wine when Pliny noted how well it had lasted:
200 years

Wine Enthusiast

Number of species of oak found worldwide.

400

Number of species used in making oak barrels.

20

The Underground Wine Journal

"… WHEN A MAN DRINKS, HE IS RICH,
EVERYTHING HE TOUCHES SUCCEEDS, HE GAINS
LAWSUITS, IS HAPPY AND HELPS HIS FRIENDS."

— *Aristophanes*

In 1996, total California wine shipments
(in gallons) surpassed this number for the first time:

400 million

Wine Business Insider

Traditional vine spacing used by most wineries in the 1980s:

454 vines per acre

Close spacing used by some wineries in the 1990s:
2,500 vines per acre

Wines & Vines

In Napa County, this varietal became the first California
grape to bring growers an average of over $1 per pound:

Cabernet Sauvignon

Wines & Vines

The single largest purchaser of fine wine in the U.S. is:

Costco

WineBusiness.com

Located in Portugal, the world's most productive
cork oak tree produces enough cork each harvest for:

100,000 wine bottles

Decanter

Oak cooperage and the grape were both introduced
to the U.S. in the 1600s by settlers from which country?

Britain

The Underground Wine Journal

Ratio of dessert wine to table wine production 50 years ago:

4.61 to 1

Wines & Vines

Following the publication of research that showed moderate wine consumption may prevent heart-related illness, wine imports to Korea rose how much in a single year?

56 percent

(Imports of Chilean wine alone surged by 148 percent.)

With one-third of all cork forests in the world Portugal supplies what percentage of the cork used in the U.S.?

85-90

A growing number of winemakers say they are enhancing mouthfeel and wine color through what procedure?

A process dubbed "micro-ox" or micro-oxygenation

(Which introduces extremely small bubbles of oxygen into fermenting wine)

Experimental software will soon allow winemakers to
check what from anywhere in the world?

How fermentation is going San Mateo County Times

Average age of a French oak tree
harvested for use in wine barrels:

170 years Demptos Napa Valley Cooperage

Chardonnay will soon perform double duty as a
drink and a what if microbiologists have their way?

A disinfectant spray Decanter.com

The planting of vineyards expressly for
winemaking dates back how many years?

8,000 Wine Spectator

Per capita spending on wine in the U.S. increased
this much between 1990 and 1998:

100%

Napa Valley Register

Balsamina, Entournerien, Chira, Hignin (Noir)
and Serenne are synonyms for which grape?

Syrah

Wine Enthusiast

Moderate drinking (one to two glasses per day) can be
as good for the heart as doing what for an hour a day?

Exercising

The New York Times

U.S. consumers who prefer to receive their
wines through the mail can sign up with approximately
how many wine clubs nationwide?

800

San Francisco Chronicle

What device have Korean scientists developed that they claim can
evaluate wine and food better than humans?

An electric tongue

Korea Herald

Top price recently paid for Napa Valley vineyard acreage:

$350,000 per acre

Wine Spectator

Women have more of these than men:

Taste buds

FineWin

Spain is the number one wine importer to what country?

China

Wines & Vines

One of India's leading vintners avoids the summertime grape-killing heat by doing what?

Growing and harvesting during winter

Contra Costa Times

Researchers now say that the Croatian wine variety Crljenak is the same as what other?

Zinfandel

Decanter

Year in which Americans bought more premium wine than jug wine for the first time in history:

1998

Barron's

"THE DISCOVERY OF A WINE
IS OF GREATER MOMENT THAN
THE DISCOVERY OF A CONSTELLATION.
THE UNIVERSE IS TOO FULL OF STARS."

— *Benjamin Franklin*

Danish researchers say that wine drinkers have
a higher what than beer drinkers or abstainers?

IQ

WineSpectator.com

Area associated with the origin of Cabernet Sauvignon:

Caspian Sea region

The Wine News

The humble grape banned in France found to
be the parent of Chardonnay:

Gouais Blanc

Napa Valley Register

Increase in red wine sales after the November, 1995
"60 Minutes" broadcast on the "French Paradox"
of apparent health benefits of drinking wine:

26%

Wine Business Insider

The cross pollination of Cabernet Franc and
Sauvignon Blanc that resulted in Cabernet
Sauvignon occurred how many years ago?

300-400

The New York Times

Date phylloxera was first discovered in California:

August 19, 1873

Winemaking in California

Amount of wine contained in a Melchior:

24 bottles (18 liters)   *Vineyard and Winery Management*

Amount of wine saved each year through lessened evaporation by keeping the barrels in a cave rather than a cellar:

6 bottles per barrel   *Elias Fernandez. Shafer Vineyards*

Commissioned for a millennium celebration, the largest bottle of Champagne ever made boasts this capacity:

120 liters   *Santé*

Two British men were arrested in the Argentinean town of Moron when police discovered they were dissolving what into wine prior to export?

250 grams of cocaine per bottle before smuggling the wine to Britain and Spain   *UPI*

This wine was the "darling of the wine industry" in 1949:

Muscatel

Wines & Vines

According to a French study, men who drink
two glasses of wine every day after suffering a
heart attack significantly cut their risk of what?

Another heart attack

The Daily Telegraph (London)

Product which rivaled wine in establishing
Napa Valley's fame in the 1880s:

Cream of Tartar

*(Produced both from grape pomace and the crystallized
sediment in wine casks, cream of tartar is used in a variety
of products, from baking powder to the rayon used for
parachutes and tents during World War II.)*

Napa Valley Register

A spa in Ontario Canada is offering a new massage ointment, which is a gooey blend of honey and what?

Chardonnay

The Standard (St. Catharines)

Estimated number of gallons of wine lost in the 1906 San Francisco earthquake:

30 million

Winemaking in California

The robust red wines of Sardinia are now believed to account for that island's unusual number of what?

Residents over the age of 100

The Financial Times

The world's largest wine collection at sea,
50,000 bottles, is claimed by what ship?

The Queen Mary 2

The World of Fine Wine

Varietal commanding the highest average price
per ton in Napa County in 2003:

Petit Verdot, $5,034/ton
(Just five years earlier this varietal sold for $2,658/ton.)

Napa County Agricultural Crop Report

Sherry comes from southern Spain where it starts as a
white wine made from the palomino grape but for
reasons unknown goes on to produce what?

A yeast-based substance called flor, which gives the wine its unique character

The New York Times

Which varietal in 1997 finally displaced French
Colombard as California's most prolific grape?

Chardonnay

Wine Enthusiast

Number of staves in a 60-gallon wine barrel:

37

Demptos Napa Cooperage

Legal maximum blood alcohol limit in California:

0.08 g.p.l.
In most European Union nations:
0.5 g.p.l.

Dan Berger's Vintage Experiences

Average time between a vine's flowering and harvest:

100 days

Napa Valley Wine Library Report

"DRINK A GLASS OF WINE AFTER YOUR SOUP AND YOU STEAL A RUBLE FROM YOUR DOCTOR."

— *Russian proverb*

Spanish researchers say that men who drink
red wine have to worry less about cancer where?

The prostate

WineSpectator.com

Planted vineyard land typically costs in Napa Valley:

$70,000 – $250,000 per acre

Wine & Spirits

Rolling Stones guitarist Keith Richards likes to
pair what with wine for breakfast?

Eggs

The New York Post

North Carolina's state fruit is what?

A wine grape called Scuppernong

The Business Journal (Greensboro, NC)

True or False: Mad Fish, Piping Shrike, Woop Woop, Fifth Leg, Jester and Boonaroo are all hip-hop terms for a popular French champagne.

False, all are wine names from Australia

Baltimore Sun

The Moldovan city of Cricova lays claim to the world's largest underground what?

Winery
(With a 40-mile labyrinth of wine-storage tunnels)

Los Angeles Times

Storing wine for 15 years at 73°F is equivalent
to how many years of aging at 55°F?

120 years

The Alchemist's Wine Perspective

Probable vintage of the first Cabernet Sauvignon
produced in California, from vines grown in
what is now the center of Los Angeles:

1837

The Wine Spectator's California Bible

In Sweden, 45 percent of all wine is
packaged in what type of container?

Boxes

Tri Valley Herald

Number of grape vines per household Virginia settlers
were ordered to plant in a 1623 colonial decree:

10

American Beverage Institute

Number of grape varieties grown in Napa County in 2003:

80
In 1880: 400

Napa County Agricultural Crop Report & Winemaking in California

---

Primary fruit crop in Napa Valley during the 1940s:

Prunes *Napa Valley Register*

Optimum temperature for photosynthesis by grape leaves:

77°F

Temperature at which photosynthesis ceases:
113°F *General Viticulture, A.J. Winkler et al.*

A glass or two of wine a day is now thought to prevent what?

Growth of polyps in the colon *Reuters*

Archeologists believe they may have found the home of Bacchus
(god of wine) in a 4th century B.C. temple located where?

Southern Bulgaria   Sofia News Agency

Average humidity in caves used for storing wine:

98%   San Francisco Chronicle

Although alcohol is banned in Iran, what group of
Iranian citizens is exempt from this prohibition?

Armenian Christians, who are allowed to make their own wine for church services

Associated Press

In 1946, Americans drank an average of two gallons
of wine per year. By what year did that double?

1980

Wine Institute

According to Harvard researchers, stress on a vine, such as
drought or lack of nitrogen can raise the content of resveratrol (a
substance credited with health benefits) in its fruit. The report
mentioned which two countries as producing stressed-out fruit?

Chile and Australia

Newsfactor.com

To tell the difference between a great old wine and
a bottle of vinegar before pulling a cork, what
kind of technology can wine lovers now turn to?

MRI scanners

The Guardian (London)

Top three countries in terms of liters per person
per year wine consumption:

Luxembourg (63.33)
France (58.15)
Italy (53.44)
**_(At 7.69 liters per person, the U.S. ranks 34th,
just edging out Latvia for that position.)_**   Wine Institute

Following a crackdown on intoxicated drivers and a 15 percent
decline in wine sales at restaurants, the French wine industry
is mounting an effort to do what?

**_Convince drivers that it's OK to have two or
three drinks before heading home_**   MSNBC

The Copenhagen heart study of more than 13,000
men and women credits moderate wine consumption
with reducing heart disease mortality by this percent:

_50_   Wine Institute

"I HAVE ENJOYED GREAT HEALTH AT A GREAT AGE
BECAUSE EVERY DAY SINCE I CAN REMEMBER
I HAVE CONSUMED A BOTTLE OF WINE
EXCEPT WHEN I HAVE NOT FELT WELL.
THEN I HAVE CONSUMED TWO BOTTLES."

— *Bishop of Seville*

One out of a hundred people is:

Sulfite-sensitive *Food and Drug Administration*

Number of wineries in Napa Valley in 2002:

250
In 1960: 25 *BATF & Napa Valley Vintners*

True or False:10 minutes after having a drink,
15 percent of the alcohol is in your bloodstream.

False, it's 50 percent *BBC*

Discovered among the buildings in Pompeii buried
by the eruption of Mt. Vesuvius in 79 A.D.:

200 wine bars

Wine Spectator

Number of 750ml bottles needed to fill a nebuchadnezzar:

15 – 20

Napa Valley Vintners

Percentage of wine produced in California
that comes from Napa Valley:

4

Sunset

The gap between the level of wine in a bottle and
the bottom of the cork is called what?

Ullage

In ancient Rome, hangover victims might attempt
to alleviate their aches and pains by:

Eating fried canaries

What nobleman of the past was buried with wine,
labeled with the year of production, the maker's name
and comments on quality?

The Egyptian Pharaoh Tutankhamun

Sulfites produced by the body each day are equivalent
to the amount present in this much wine:

100 bottles

The German government has denounced an Italian
wine that bears the likeness of whom on its labels?

Adolph Hitler

News.com.au

Brain scans conducted on sommeliers while drinking wine
showed increased activity in the frontal cortex, an area of the
brain used for thinking. Casual drinkers showed activity where?

The amygdala, the part of the brain
that reacts to pleasure

Quarterly Review of Wines

How many grape growers make their living from the appellations
of the regions of Beaujolais and Beaujolais Villages?

4,000

Winnipeg Sun

Some vintners in England are predicting what phenomenon
will aid their efforts to produce more and better quality
wine grape varieties?

Global warming

Associated Press

Fifty years ago just 4% of Britons did it.
Today it's nearer to 74%. What has gained such popularity?

Drinking wine

The Guardian (London)

The major oak species in France are: Quercus robur and Quercus
sessiliflora. In America the major white oak for barrels is:

Quercus alba

Wine Business Monthly

Number of hours a cork needs to regain
its full size after extraction:

24

Knowing & Making Wine, E. Peynaud

Percentage of Napa County planted to vineyards:

9

Napa Valley Vintners

Bottles of wine purchased by Thomas Jefferson
during the eight years of his presidency:

20,000

Passions: The Wines and Travels of Thomas Jefferson

Number of vine-damaging gophers one pair of
barn owls and their young can consume each year:

1,000

Practical Winery & Vineyard

Number of acres of Cabernet Sauvignon in Napa Valley in 1950:

150
In 2003: 17,458

The Wine Atlas of California & Napa County Agricultural Crop Report

When market researchers asked U.S. wine consumers
to name wine's number one attribute, they said:

"Makes a good gift"   *Wine Market Council*

True or False: In Victorian England, mulled
wine was considered a health drink.

True   *San Francisco Chronicle*

Number of wineries in California when Prohibition began:

700
Number of wineries today:
1049   *Santa Rosa Press Democrat & MKF Research*

"THERE IS NO DOUBT THAT NOT TO DRINK WINE
IS A GREAT DEDUCTION FROM LIFE."

— *James Boswell quoting Samuel Johnson*

As early as 4,000 B.C. these were the first
people to use corks as stoppers:

Egyptians

St. Helena Star

Number of U.S. states that have wineries:

50

WineAmerica.org

Harvard School of Public Health says women who
drink one to two glasses of wine per day may
lower their risk of developing what?

Type 2 Diabetes

Quarterly Review of Wines

Waste water from a nuclear power plant is warming the soil, allowing this country to produce wine for the first time:

Finland

Ananova.com

True or False: From 1995 to 2002, per person wine consumption in China rose 12 percent.

False, it rose 53 percent

The New York Times

Average number of bottles of Champagne or sparkling wine a cellar worker is expected to riddle (turn) by hand each day:

50,000

Classic Methods Classic Varieties (CMCV)

You can take this drug or you can drink wine regularly to
get heart-protecting anti-clotting in the bloodstream.

Aspirin

Newsweek

The *governo* method used in the Chianti region, involves
harvesting grapes, then setting them aside to do what?

Dry

*(The dried fruit is later pressed, and its
unfermented juice is added to wine.)*

WineSpectator.com

In 1984, the federal government threatened to cut
highway funding to states that refused to do what?

Raise their drinking age to 21   San Francisco Chronicle

Country which is the largest wine importer in the world:

Germany

Global Wine News e-Monitor

Bordeaux produces how much wine a year?

6.5 million hectoliters (171.7 million gallons)

Wall St. Journal

Napa County acreage planted to grapes in 2003:

44,074 acres
To wheat in 1868: 97,000 acres

Napa County Agricultural Crop Report & Napa Valley Register

True or False: In France AOCs (appellation d'origine controlie) mandate which grape varieties may be used and dictate how to clearly spell out this information on the label.

False

(AOCs generally ban winemakers from
including this information on the label.)

Agence France-Presse

Italian vintners are recreating the wines of what lost civilization?

**Pompeii, whose vineyards last
produced wine in 79 A.D.**   *Decanter.com*

Estimated number of taste buds located on the human tongue:

10,000

California State University at Chico & The American Wine Society Journal

---

Hungary's famed botrytized sweet wine
Tokay is traditionally made from:

Furmint, Harslevelu and Muscat   *WineSpectator.com*

California is the leading state in wine consumption in the U.S., with more than 42 million cases of wine sold a year. What state is a distant second?

New York (19 million cases sold) Wine Market Council

Number of varieties of wine grapes existing worldwide:

10,000 Wine for Dummies

In the late 1860s, growers in the Rhône Valley hoped to bring a divine halt to the onslaught of phylloxera by bringing the bones of what saint from Rome to a local church?

St. Valentine Belfast Telegraph

Estimated number of wine corks in use worldwide today:

11 billion Wines & Vines

The premiere wine-growing area of Austria is called Lower Austria. To locate this region on a map of that country, where should you look?

In the upper right corner (or the northeast)

Detroit Free Press

Approximate number of grape clusters that go into a bottle of wine:

Three

Shafer Vineyards

The term "reserve" on wine labels first appeared in what year?

1933

(The year Prohibition ended, when Beaulieu Vineyards introduced its Private Reserve Napa Valley Cabernet)

The Daytona Beach News-Journal

France has 466 appellations. The U.S. has how many?

154

The Chicago Wine School

"MORE MIRACLES COME FROM A CASK FULL OF
WINE THAN A CASK FULL OF SAINTS."

— *Italian Proverb*

Researchers report some success in controlling
levels of blood sugar with what three substances?

Coffee, cinnamon and wine

ScienceNews.org

True or False: a papsakke is a the name
of a Korean version of Sake.

False
(It is a South African five-liter foil bag of wine.)

AllAfrica.com

A mechanical harvester can pick
how many tons of grapes a day?

100

The Paris News (Texas)

Researchers say that grape growers who lose tonnage to hungry European starlings may soon find relief thanks to:

Garlic oil

(Which is showing promise as an environmentally safe starling repellent) *Associated Press*

Most of Michigan's wine grapes grow within 25 miles of:

Lake Michigan

MichiganWines.com

Cigars, toy robots, a deer head and expensive wines were all listed in a recent report as illegal purchases by whom?

U.S. government employees armed with Uncle Sam's credit cards

Reuters

What is the key difference between Nebraska wineries and those in Napa Valley, according to published remarks by a University of Nebraska professor of horticulture and viticulture?

Proper marketing

LaVistaSun.com

If you're drinking a red wine from the small South American country of Uruguay, you're probably quaffing Tannat, a grape brought over 250 years ago by:

Basque settlers

TheWineLoversPage.com

The U.S. government has granted wine producers the opportunity to add the term "low carbohydrate" to wines that contain no more than seven grams of carbohydrate per serving. Under these rules, what percentage of dry wines (as opposed to dessert wines) qualify for this new designation?

100%

WineLoversPage.com

London merchants who bottled wines in the 18th century blended what with their Bordeaux wines to increase the Bordeaux's appeal and value?

Rhone's Syrah

The Star (Malaysia)

In a poll of U.S. single adults, 35 percent of men said what trait makes women more attractive?

Knowledge and passion about wine

OnlineDatingMagazine.com

A Lutheran minister in Wisconsin is petitioning lawmakers to allow believers behind bars to partake of what?

Real wine for holy communion
(instead of grape juice)

Associated Press

What do grapes have in common with acorns,
walnuts, coffee, tea, apples, and pears?

All contain tannins *Visalia Times-Delta*

Better than industry statistics, perhaps most telling
of wine's growing popularity in the U.S. is a new wine festival
in Nashville, Tennessee that offers:

Wine tastings, cooking demonstrations and tours of a NASCAR racetrack called the Superspeedway, where the event is held *Tennessean.com (Nashville)*

In Kentucky farmers are planting vineyards
to replace what traditional crop?

Tobacco *Philadelphia Inquirer*

A French company is marketing a new gadget called a diffuser which plugs into a home computer and can do what?

Reproduce an endless variety of smells offered via the Internet, including that of wine
(swirl and sip not included)

Scotsman.com

True or False. Wines have been produced in New Mexico since the 1920s.

False
Since 1629, 150 years before the first wine grape was planted in California

Detroit Free Press

Fifty percent of respondents to a U.S. poll said one should spend how much on a bottle of wine for a first date?

$15

OnlineDatingMagazine.com

Before the continent was called America in 1507, it had been given what other name by 10th century European explorers?

Wineland

(a.k.a. Vinland, by 10th century Norse explorers who were impressed by the abundance of wild grape vines) The Vinland Sagas

On May 25 each year millions of French city dwellers engage in "Operation House Party," an annual tradition of sharing a bottle of wine with whom?

Their neighbors Sydney Morning Herald

The Italian producer of a wine that bears Bob Dylan's signature, gets together with the legendary singer how often to test the wines, visit the vineyards and discuss winemaking issues?

Never

(The vintner has not met singer and works solely with Dylan's manager mostly via email) Belfast Telegraph

"IF YOU WISH TO GROW THINNER, DIMINISH YOUR DINNER, AND TAKE TO LIGHT CLARET INSTEAD OF PALE ALE."

— *Henry Leigh, "On Corpulence"*

In response to the French government's crack down on drinking and driving, one vintner has responded by producing a bottle that is the equivalent of two glasses of wine and it is called:

Permis de Conduire or "Permit to Drive"
(The label design even mimics the look of a French driver's license)

WineSpectator.com

The naturally occurring chemical compound Methoxy pyrazine in wine grapes is responsible for the flavor of:

Bell peppers

San Francisco Chronicle

California wineries play host to how many visitors a year?

14 million
Sacramento Bee

Researchers say that older people who drink a moderate amount of wine suffer less from:

Hearing loss

Wines & Vines

Women who drink wine with dinner are half as likely as nondrinkers to be what?

Obese

Rocky Mountain News

The world's wine producers have a new weapon, atomic spectrometry (which can identifying the unique "fingerprint" of 16 trace elements present in a wine), to fight what?

Fraud

The Independent (London)

True or False: The term "reserve" on a wine label has legal meaning only in France and the United States.

False

(It only has legal meaning in Spain and Italy, where it refers to wine that is specially aged prior to release)

The Daytona Beach News-Journal

About a quarter of people are born with more taste buds than others, giving them heightened sensitivity, especially to bitterness. These people are known as:

Super tasters

San Jose Mercury News

Scientists have found evidence that grape vines have been on earth at least how long?

Fossil vines have been discovered dating back 60 million years

WinePros.org

Researchers in England say that restaurant patrons spend
more money on dinner and order pricier wines when:

Classical music plays in the background

Quarterly Review of Wine

Priced at $500,000, the most expensive bottle *never* sold
was a Thomas Jefferson-owned Margaux 1787.
Why was it never auctioned off?

A waiter at a New York hotel bearing a coffee tray bumped into and broke it *Rocky Mountain News*

According to investment experts, great wines from great
vintages show what kind of annual percentage increases
over the past 40 years?

Less than ten percent *The Guardian (U.K.)*

Australian vintners are putting hopes that a 4mm microchip —
or a series of them connected wirelessly — placed in their
vineyards will do what?

Signal them when conditions are right for certain kinds of mold

Electronic News

An Australian researcher found that bottles of wine sold
faster when they were decorated by what?

A gold sticker

The Sunday Mail (Brisbane)

First person to graft French vines onto American
rootstock to prevent phylloxera:

Texas viticulturalist T.V. Munson

Wine Spectator

What is Jesus Juice?

**A nickname for white wine made famous
by singer Michael Jackson**

CBSNews.com